THE LEAF PATH

THE LEAF PATH

poems by Emily Warn

Copper Canyon Press : Port Townsend 1982

ACKNOWLEDGMENT to the following magazines, where some of these poems have appeared: *Amphora Review*, *Calyx*, *The Floating Poetry Gallery*, *Northwest Oasis*, *Pigiron*, *The Seattle Review*, *The Seattle Times* (Poetry Seattle), *Willow Springs*, *Xanadu*.

Copper Canyon Press acknowledges the assistance of a grant from the National Endowment for the Arts. Special thanks to Centrum, where Copper Canyon is Press-in-residence.

King County Arts Commission
Publications Project, 1981 Selection
Susan Griffin, juror

ISBN 0-914742-61-2

Copper Canyon Press
Box 271
Port Townsend, WA 98368

Copper Canyon Press acknowledges the assistance of a grant from the National Endowment for the Arts.
Special thanks to Centrum, where Copper Canyon is Press-in-residence.

FOR CAROLYN ALLEN

For Carolyn,
Dancing like a bomb abroad,
our souls must meet at 3a.m.
Love,
Emily

CONTENTS ✢

One

Two

Three

ONE

We walked arm in arm leaving a late film,
the streets damp, the traffic lights in full motion
in the tail winds of a storm.
Without thought our lips brushed
linked by the film's helpless hope;
the bittersweet bread those men harvested
as the clouds tore at the wheat.
At my work, the wind carrying memories
of the storm in under the window cracks,
I think of my carelessness;
the window sills not caulked,
the rings left from steaming cups of tea
and I wish for a keener life
threshing the last of the wheat,
linked by fear and the needs of family
as the first blizzard of winter
sweeps in from Canada, dwarfing them,
black figures huddled in acres of stubble
and drifting snow.
At my desk, I sense the weather
and forget, glimpse love as our lips met
and forget, but I understand these moments
come to be memories I use in my work.
Each task is the same wish to plant
the yellowest seed on earth,
the one that blooms at 4 a.m.
wakened by wind.
Words revered as joints, pulleys,
wheelbarrows carting in dirt and mulch,
carting off broken stalks, useless straw.
Words revered as messengers of our common work.

By the gate to your house
I listen to the light rain
dampening the weathered fence.
I walked all morning to arrive here.
The back alley, empty of people,
fills with wet bricks and the humming
of birds.   I wait for you to appear
in the glass sky of your door,
your face caught in a net of branches.
The grey sky soothes.
It links the bare alder and scrawny city firs.
Everything came clear
when I said I loved you more than loving.
Those words   protected seeds   thin shelled.
There is in you   in me
    two souls that want to know.
I cannot help you.
I cannot rinse the ashen color from your eyes.
But step out, open your door.
The back alleys grow ivy for warmth
                    and streaked wood.
The rain beads the dullest brown leaves.
Let us walk until our faces are windows.

I do not know the name
of the white bloom under the eucalyptus;
its blowsy petals move slowly as old age.
The eucalyptus trees clack in the wind,
their quill shaped leaves rub their dry skins,
scour the air with piney scent.
In all this shifting shadow,
I pause open-mouthed as the flower,
at the pattern of light and dark
last year's ivy makes with its new leaves.
Their uplifted thin green matches
the waving clover whose three heart-shaped leaflets
float on the air like kelp buoys,
letting each swell slide beneath them.
I scoop a handful of threadlike stems
dangling down to their dirt anchors,
crush their sour sweetness in my mouth.
It is an involuntary motion,
a taste I learned as a child.

Phillip Schultz is famous, Susie,
remember him, the mean poet at Kalamazoo College,
the one who x'ed out your sweet corn
but liked the poem about the star we pocketed
at Lowell Street cemetery in late November.
I, in my red down jacket, dirty from smoke
and the flailed dreams of summer
when I first named the stars—Cassiopeia,
Andromeda, Altair—that you scaled
with laughter. You wore scrubbed hand-me-downs,
perfume from bottles in a careful order
we swept apart. We walked across frozen ground
under big elms, the stars lingered
in the branches, we opened our jackets,
forgetting to breathe in the dark.

For James Wright

At dusk beside my father's camper
I was so small
the eucalyptus trees rustled safety.
Naked in the morning I sat on the mud bank
cuffing water spiders, browsing miner's lettuce.
The creek rippled past an upright branch
staking the sun in its exact center.
The next time I thought to look
I was twelve at the end of Ten Mile Road in Detroit.
I had walked for miles in the rain
past brick ranchettes, scooped out lots, slick traffic
searching for an empty field with tall grass
where I could hide my small breasts,
my hips wide as circular driveways.
My pockets bulged with roadside flowers—
rusted bolts, glass, chrome pieces.
Near the Ford Freeway I found
the thick trunk of a dying elm
to shelter me and a sparrow balanced
on the drooping branch of a honeysuckle.
As for now
I rest so easy in my clothes
I turn my face away,
my clearest moments spent stifling the impulse
to become everything I walk past:
sails veering on the Bay,
stink of piss in benches on the pier,
fish flopping, someone's foot on the arching scales.

Esther hunches under a juniper;
little girls shriek in the shrubbery.
They have never seen her eerie species
covered with juniper bark and dirt.
Her own song stuck, she cannot echo
the children mimicking birds.
A blackbird signals her past,
her wooden childhood among ghosts
ballooning like uncontrollable words.
No settled roosts, no hen house,
Esther sits in her clumsy blind
waiting to leap, her soul on her skin,
her ghosts whirling in the children's eyes.

Esther woke empty
from worry and no rest,
not one reason for living.
After days without bread and water,
without conversation,
without the smooth skin under arms,
spirits have stopped talking to her at night.
She woke and hurried from her small ambitions,
half-cracked.
The grey ghost of herself
lost in her dreamless nights calls and calls
caught between two limits: love and love;
the invisible spirit life she can remember
only at the cost of lovely woman's thighs.

Esther sits all day by a lake,
a can of worms and bread,
emptying rusty pipes for crayfish
to catch carp. She watches
their mud hives in shallow water, waiting.
The ice shacks are gone
along with the bourbon drinkers
stooping over their holes all winter.
Esther snags one whiskery catfish
and a bag of cocaine.
She watches and waits
until the souls of old rabbis and recent lovers
gape fisheyed at her luminescent worms.
She watches the blue sky enter her hands
and tug a skeleton into the air.
She slips salmon eggs into its sunken eyes,
pierces its earless skull with trout flies
and plasters on a wig of worms.
Esther casts the mossy bones
dancing into the waves.
The grey ghost of herself claps and claps.

The day sits in Esther's lap
waiting to be cross hatched
like water in the wake of purse seiners.
Already the sun ransacked the path
wet with rose hips and ferns.
Exhausted by smells of home, her island,
Esther leans against cloth walls.
She ran across two continents,
the wolf and loon sang back
to the heap and swell of cold waters
in the north, where memory bit.
She disguised her love as a pearl
she hid under pulp log fires,
nursed with a stick, charred she claimed,
to write with.
The slow accretion of moons
lowered themselves to the sea
snapped her eyes away,
a night creature guarding her secret with a circle
of small fires roaring on the beach, bats leaped
across; loons clapped, wolves
came near enough to smell.
A cedar branch in the shape of a woman
bore no mark of human hands,
a box of flame,
a skiff winds follow.

When the lake froze, Esther wrapped her pearl
in bearded moss, placed it in two clam shells
under her waist where it ripened as she walked.
The marine air welcomed her,
but her lover's arms never opened.
Wolves called to her,

but her legs grown heavy with nights
drinking milk and eating
could not carry her back
to dancing in the ashes of lost loves.
Her lover was herself,
a secret she never could share.
She carried a single grain of sand
in her eye
to remember old fires.

Legendary Esther walks invisible,
trying to seize her life separate
from her funny sex. She sniffs marigolds
in traffic, catches the eyes of trees
to guide her through the oak forest.
She walks in dry air on a rainy day,
impervious, following her own scent.
Under the river poplars, Esther leaves no tracks
when she tames the killdeer's bent wing,
their young are in no danger from her wild eyes
seeing nothing that is there. Beyond, in her mind,
the sages rustle against elderberry,
against chia and green rushes by the small creeks.
By instinct, Esther returns each spring
to the boulder strewn narrow to watch swallows
re-work the cliff side, flying from the mud bottom
to their high nests, building their kivas.
Esther hurries up the mountain, scrambling
in the dry oak leaves and loose dirt.
Scared grouse boom in time with her heart
against the heat and the dry fear
that her god will call and she will not hear.
Esther grabs young pines and pulls herself
to the wide plateau. Flower after flower
after flower orange on the green rounded mountain,
the hot pines and creek veins invisible.
Esther stands dead tired on the edge,
the sky bright with clouds,
every leaf of grass green and breathing.

gone all summer from view
          inland
feeding in the dying birch
swamps, where thimbleberry grows thick
          as his matted shedding coat.

He browses on young firs,
          wild plums,
alder, utterly disdain-
ful of the spruce, the bristled-cotton
          of thimbleberry leaves, of

vines sticky with spittle,
          species
abundant on a fifty
square mile island where eight hundred
          moose each eat forty veg-

etable pounds per day.
          He shrugs
his thatched large head and achieves
a world's underwater breath record
          siphoning sulphurous

weeds with a full set of
          antlers,
stirring the bottom plants with-
in tongue's reach. Occasional
          cows signal from the coast.

He continues eating
          sometimes
joining the nocturnal trade

route of a cow and calf, sharing
in the brisk fir gossip

listening for clues. Their
pace is
too frantic, too keen for alder plumes,
for one who knows the world's largest
beaver dam is in Siskwit

Bay, twenty-five feet tall,
a pond
muddy, deep, stagnant, he can
feed all fall, water covering his
neck. He keeps his secret.

I walk my morning beat.
Steam blinds the cafe windows.
A starling caws at the slow sun
nodding behind the city reservoir,
where two cops, like shoes placed heel
to toe in a box, chat in their cars.
On mornings like these, I envy their quota
of tickets, envy anyone with measurable work:
the truck farmer with his produce,
the espresso peddler,
the broker with his graph of careful guesses.
I cannot say,
rinse the dirt from these green words,
they will nourish you, or,
mark the rise and fall of these lines,
note the stable sounds that repeat,
you will profit from them.
I cannot even promise addiction.

They changed the numbers of the bus routes.
The Number Ten no longer climbs the hill
past Terrestrial Views Art Gallery
and the shop window filled with chandeliers.
They scrambled all the vistas.
Gas Works Park is now on the shore
of Puget Sound.
Numbers lost their neighborhoods,
lost their names.
I no longer can say,
there goes a man from the Forty-Three, a Swede.
Someone else's face opens and shuts
like his, tending the locks he imagined
as he rode to and from the canals.
Women loaded with packages
curse oddly instead of evenly.
Drunks board the Free Ride
and end up in the yards of the rich
unable to find their way back downtown.

The bus to the ferry
travels far inland.
Mirages shine between traffic
and the driver blinded by years
of late sun on water.
He swerves to miss a taxi
thinking it is a slow tug.
Nurses past midnight
in the bowery district
frantic for their bus
watch the street open
like a draw bridge.
Tall masts glide past,

they ask the man in the crow's nest,
Has he seen the nine,
The Number Nine,
Number Nine,
Number Nine,
Number Nine. . . .

I'm on the wrong street.
The corner store graffiti boasts
curses of unfamiliar gangs.
Two blocks away,
the Great Highway escorts the sea,
exhaust carpeting the dune grass.
I cannot get across.
From this distance, the sea's gaudy blue
matches The Mar Motel sign;
it is the same color my grandmother chose
for my Yom Kippur dress.
I will not brag about my tribe.
They slit my tongue
when I wanted to lead the singing.
Only men could praise God
with those lilting, mournful tunes.
I donned by brother's tzitzis,
pinned up my hair,
and wrapped my grandfather's tefilum
in spirals around my arm.
I talked with God, whispering in sacred Hebrew,
naming the four corners of the world
where Jews thump their hearts,
mine pounded with shame
knowing God heard me thank Him
for letting me be a man.

For my grandfather (1901-1976)

It is still Shabbas. As soon as three stars
join the moon you pour wine and dovin. I hold
the Havdalah candle as high as my wished for
husband, the six strands of light trembling
with the tenor of your Hebrew words.

Afterwards, each Saturday night, you lit your best
schnapps in a shallow bowl, let the yellow flame
lick your fingers, and then snuffed your gold
hands in your trousers rejoicing, "Money burns
a hole in your pocket."

You downed one shot wishing us, "Gut Vuch!
Gut Vuch!" The amyl nitrate you hid
in every cupboard listened to your credulous
heart for thirty years.

Level with the edge of the gully,
a bird preens in the towering elms
sampling each of its songs for the sound
that will repeat and vary the morning,
like rain distinguishing itself from rain
by falling on the broken gutter,
like the names of God—I suppose
although writing His most popular name
I want to burn the paper scrap
in the holy bin at synagogue.
The uninitiated should not sound the unwritten forms.
The bird flies off.
I heard nothing
but some voice repeating old poems
as if memory aligns the soul,
as if memory unravels codes of bird songs,
glyphs, ivy spiralling the oak.
Nothing can be known by reason.
All first principles are proven by listening.
O Hear O Hear O Israel
more than one O strummed together is not O.
Yet I sound gods, faith and memory
as if I knew something,
as if those words changed what I did:
walked past a few quiet pines
up a steep back street
embossed with damp granite rock gardens and ferns
to where that inevitable bird crowning
the houses lost me in the invisible branches.

1928-1973

In Cheyenne I posted poems
on tavern doors asking for Jack Warn.
The men who drink to forget
the desolate bluffs that finish each street
think of my words as the used Harley for sale,
or the five acres south of town
with trailer and corner stream.
It is nine years since my father and I drove
through the stunted mountains to Laramie.
The men know that road, their first drunks
were there, they know how the yellow line
escorted by headlights tunnels into darkness,
how the scrawny pines point out Wyoming
to the moon. We stopped at every ranch
and tavern to celebrate my return
after fifteen years. At the Silver Bell Saloon
we talked, but were too drunk
to remember our words.
Six months later he was dead;
the brilliant boy who left Cheyenne
to look for love and a full horizon
and found both until war and his gnawing
childhood seared his brain.
He returned to Wyoming's emptiness,
to frame a final honest gesture
by burying himself in snow
one block from his home.

Two women in linen shirts,
reedy and full of birds,
pick shore weeds and gossip.
A recluse stalks their laughter.
His hungers leave him.
This is why he came
down from the moutains
to hear talk of stealing tea
from under the empress's sharp
pointed nails, and of the river god.
They run to the wooden boats,
watch the current for sea otters
that have come this far
to open their pores with rain
and the greens of fresh water plants.
On the bow slats they string bamboo beads
into long skirts, pound weeds into dyes,
compose fantastic scenes
on the empress's silk shirts:
a sandpiper's slender legs
printed in fluvial sand,
river gorges of light bend
in calm rapids. It is delicate work
making the gods live again.

TWO

Lady Murasaki walks down Broadway
in the early morning, her kimono soiled,
one of her butterfly's wings torn from listening
to a man loving her lover.
Cooing and chortling pigeons,
in the gutter are deeper pleasures.
She smokes jugum in the rain
while the birds are singing.
Walks at the crest of the city
while the sun sets behind the crest
of another world.
She never sighs.
She laughs at the poor
and gives them her old beans,
the shoes in the back of her closet,
lets them into her kitchen
to smell tarragon and parsley
in her potato soup.
Lets them ride with her,
wind in their hair and bluegrass
tugging at their feet to be dancing
in between buildings in the one square of sunlight.
Lady Murasaki's lover waits for her
at a corner and says it was boring.
Lady Murasaki knows different;
she heard their duet;
she wanted to be in both of their arms.

Lady Murasaki competes with birds
for high wire arabesque.
She climbs her perch, her spurs rap the pole.
She clips her gold and purple finger nails
to copper boxes, places lines between her teeth
and hums sonatas in minor keys.
For weeks she listened to operator's pitch,
the tone of time and push button scales
to crack the code and open the wires.
The cables jangle gossip and local news;
Lady Murasaki interrupts with melody,
bending rhythm and blues to Omaha,
railroad songs to Philly.
She whistles the code in nursery rhyme.
They chime in with tips: word of mouth jobs,
places to live, lessons in graft.
Happy to be heard, she arias loud and long,
relaying what counts: collect solitary roosts,
invent your own keys, tour the past.
Like frightened pigeons they click off.
The dial tones gather like lint on her chords.

Mix flour and soda, add weak tea,
Lady Murasaki breakfasts on biscuits.
She is famished from fancy foods
                and glamorous entertainment.
The simple life, she sighs.
She is learning Vietnamese,
growing philodendrons and knitting socks.
Good credentials for her new job
welcoming the general public
to bank lobbies, twenty-six story
                view restaurants.

Her socks are coded resumes
for boat refugees and miscellaneous exiles.
When to knit   when to purl
she learns from reading business plans
and passes on the best to would be losers
who want a share in the green jungle.

No shells yet, no car bombs
                rock her bedroom.
The terrorists attack with boredom.
Her kimono sweeps the marble lobbies,
her smile is held in place with pins.
She practices Vietnamese idioms
                with newcomers,
and if they ask the name
of the lavender blooming in the ivy,
she opens her packet of seeds.

Lady Murasaki comes to the marsh
where the blackbirds sing
and waves bloom nodding over logs.
Drunk on white wine,
ladies in long skirts and straw hats,
men in pin stripes, red carnations in their wide lapels.
No real talk.
A glass of champagne keeps time
from nagging and nagging.

Who is Lady Murasaki to think she is outside
of their picnic, champagne bubbling, their pleased gaiety strained.
Bored with the literary world,
with salons biting their tails,
her work begins in an old chair and a strange room,
with her spoiled life and fear of their talk.

Did T.S. Eliot get filthy with swamp ducks?
Sit in cattails sliced with green?
Lady Murasaki watches the lake disappear
under boats. The roar of a catered life,
running a race with no finish, the line strung
and snapped by earlier war horses trampling
ancient secrets frantic with death.

Wearing his boots and a belt buckle,
Lady Murasaki walks into the bog recalling
sailor men and their wide strides breathing in the sea,
"I'd run from home, from my small berth,
if you'd let me be one of you staring
at the bright sea and mindless blue,
but add my breasts, my round breasts
and the expanse of waves drops from your sight."

Lady Murasaki picked each butterfly off her gown,
ground the wings to powder
and moved to Saskatchewan's   sky and land
                                        sky and land
and heavy work horses.
The fury of her hundred students cannot reach her.
They must teach themselves to suspend
the day's faces,
fish sewers for carp.
Lady Murasaki left clues:
tropical fruits budding
next to underground heating pipes,
their tangent rinds mix with steam
confusing her students' senses.
She is off in her stretch of still prairie,
her back planked as wooden barn windows.
She notes the endless scenery,
the wind rinsing each of her ribs
with a memory of an audible self.
Lady Murasaki sighs and stretches in the hay,
designing fritillary moth wings, spiralled cocoons,
keen antennae,   exchanging them for secrets
the wind has carried over miles of grass.

Lady Murasaki is in love,
her eyes round as aureoles.
Her last gram of sadness
dissolved in yesterday's bath.
Today the grackle's hoarse call has rhythm.
Starlings brush her study windows with iridescence.
She sits polishing her skin,
remembering how their hearts beat
on the outsides of their bodies,
how their fingers, tentative at first,
calmed and flattened their flowering veins.

What would her love say
to see her staring,
her hand turning into vines,
her memories living off memory.
For days her notebooks bloomed violets.
Silver maples appeared out of nowhere.
Her hearing fails when she recalls
the first time her love came
to her room and asked to be touched,
as when a leaf's delicate ribs
brush against the sun.

Lady Murasaki diminished;
her kimonos bagged, swayed
around her thin form.
Her butterfly's sequin eyes
dangled from loose threads;
her embroidered locust trees lost their green.
The heat refused to break.
Her moods frayed waiting for the wind's breath
to reach her from the clamoring birch.
The woodpeckers and jays squabbled
too humid to fly.
The catbird's insistent complaint
labeled summer stifling,
too loud for Lady Murasaki to admire
the pattern on the Mayfly's wing,
or the crescendo and caesura of wind
in the tall branches cajoling her to join
summer's parade of feathers: swallow tails,
tiger lilies, luna moths;
to forget the distance between her
and the waterfall tapering to a pool
lined with red lace maples, yellow iris,
tamarisked black pines that appeared
a month ago while practising her brush strokes.
She set out with walking stick
to discover its locale. Thimbleberry thicket
led to squat alder grove to scraggly dense
undergrowth. The forest failed to open,
no meadows, no swift creeks.
She gave up under a second growth pine,
ransacked her memory for songs,
none echoed off the pine's thin poles.
Only the stars at night matched her longing

for graceful distance from July's inner abandon.
She recited the waterfall's hush to sleep
and dreamed she was a lily floating, unperturbed.
She dreamed she interpreted her dream
by composing poems in the shapes of leaves:
evergreen needles, trembling poplars, gingko fans;
a leaf syllable echoed and roared
in the hollow of a thick tree, fire scarred, wide,
then fluttered and caught in the grooves of bark
spiralling upward. Lady Murasaki followed her lead,
another leaf scuttling, a ripple of green.
She woke on the highest branch unfurling
into words, spilling into the leaves.

THREE

Two crones in a rotten shack
create habits.
Their fingers mimic insects
dismantling a tree's bark
to learn xylem's secret motion.
They tend a single fire,
rise to clutter and cold,
split wood salvaged from clear cuts,
chip rust off frozen rain.
For tea savored near the stove
they share silence, look through
each other to tall firs, watch the sea
their eyes wild as the stone beach,
each rock fracturing light.
Their twin shells curved hollow
by their sister tongues,
hold fire through the long winter
and the house livid with coals.

Her eyelashes pencil in my nakedness.
Mornings next to her I can smell
the ground of her being.
When the worn tips of her fingers
smooth in my lines I cry like fog
seeping into her fields.

The world intrudes:
a flatbed truck stacked with clean lumber
rolls out of a ship's hold,
a dacron filled man totters
from his pigeon hole on the wharf.
I fit nowhere.

Mornings she brews tea; eye of moth wing,
song of wren, luring spirits into inanimate forms.
Soon we'll no longer dress like puppets
for the grinning spectacle.
No longer map mountains,
separate moss from cedar for compass sites.
We'll live within the mushrooming
forest, drink from earthenware
we have stored in our bodies.

Yesterday the meadow, the long unopened daisies,
all early summer flowers—paint brush, strawberry,
clover—were ghosts of themselves in thick fog
as I rattled past on the tractor,
the visible world a shifting sphere
with ragged perimeter: row of birch trees
curved to lines of sawtoothed grasses
changed to a drainage ditch brimming
with coral root, arrowhead, then we stopped.
The warehouse contained the circle.
Work.
By noon the sun burned through
silenced the low calls of boats
motoring down the invisible harbor.

This morning the sun swelters at 7 a.m.;
the poems I open tell about taunting lovers
who leave without looking back, untouched,
left intact by their forward motion,
their temporary anchors forgotten.
My loss is yesterday's ghostly ring;
the hot sun dispels the link
to my fog drenched home on another coast
where my lover waits. Islanded.
The mail plane lands once a week.
My days filled with forgetfulness
of hard work. At night, the dream we composed
separates. I sweep and sweep my temporary kitchen,
keep time by the woodpecker who rivets
the unraveling birch for food,
picture the half-moon of your arms as my hearth.

I lived on the coast
The year deep snow mixed with rain
And froze

We gave up travel

My desire
Was the distance between us
Smooth granite I wanted to scale

The windows glazed
In our separate houses

Can I live with a loss
Emptiness cannot fill
Until the snow melts

I poise on the edge
Again

Leaves scraping the last light
clammer and sigh to the bark
and stretch to the long red
    evening in the north.

I try to drift like the leaves,
        like the hitchhiker
decoding a diesel truck's backward nickname,
thanking cows who nod
        at the right lonely car
allowing the windfences and arching
sky to climb in the door.

I try but you accuse me
        of first degree emptiness.
I sit watching the trees.
Smoke billows into the house.
My seedpod lightness cuffed by winds
lodges in the chimney's throat.

I don't know why love fails,
why you became a tyro cowboy
corralling my drift.

It is a mean time
    with muddy wood and our drinking
water turning to ice.
Before we warmed our palms
    with proper recipes for tea,
happy that the rain
    had swept our two lives
into the first convenient shelter.

Now the nagging fire,
our waning love,
dwindles or flares.

I cannot remember your words,
only the precise fury of your voice
beating me into the kitchen corner
where I crouched cold and soundless
behind a wall suddenly tangible.

Later we slept the sleep
    of the war weary,
held on to each other's soft limbs
    to keep our failure
from roosting in our bed.

The wind roars louder.
I want to read the bottom of my own cup,
figure my stars without you.

On the night my face betrayed me
my mouth formed words I never intended.
Later, I crawled off to construction sites,
to tunnels under sewers in this large city
and slept until I tired of waiting
for you to find me. In the morning
I walked out into the tottering street
and hammered at air until my words
cleared a space filled with sea water.

Repeat after me. Do not walk through
any closed doors, skin and clothing catch
on the aching hole of your lost life.
I gained nothing by sleeping a few nights
wrapped in a woman's arms. Words ran out
of the tips of my fingers while I slept,
my body filled with images of her lines
and the trails her hands cut.

I will write a script. In the fourth act
you will leave me for him the moon
will be in Cancer. Since I know
what is coming I will be prepared.
You will forget your lines, when you look down
at your cue cards, at the lip reader in the wings,
you will know they were never written.
My own long soliloquy will be stunning.

I am writing this out of vengeance
which is a hurt given to the self
in the name of another.
                    —Tess Gallagher

I will let you go this time
without notching my wrist
one more week without air.

The weather flies its leaves and clouds.
People take their tea and papers in green rain jackets,
jeer themselves alive at football games, in taverns.

Nothing else happens.
Smoke tightens the walls of the room.
No one I know is here.

I will let you go without thinking I am letting you go,
no longer calling your lack of emotion
at the wrong times, lovely.

I will let you go for the last
and first time without blaming myself
for your silence. I will let you go.

I will be as transparent as rain
and the large hum of voices
that are wholly my own.

Nothing can shake my concentration,
not the empty coffee cup,
nor the lack of anything to say,

nor that rock, my heart,
that you shoved through glass.

A woman is lying on a sheet printed with lilies
and wild geraniums.
Her arm brushes the skeletal imprint
of a woman she kissed the first time that evening.
Under her lids, the lilies and geraniums
fuse into a hybrid scotch broom
she saw growing by the trolley tracks—
yellow sepals frilled by purple.
The evening wind off the sea
boosts fog over the hills,
thin wisps trail into her window
enlarging the ceiling into a cathedral.
She has forgotten why the evening is pleasant.
She pictures the tassled silk of corn
dusting her breasts,
a woman's lips nuzzling the pollen.
The air is scented with lavender.

Outside a rain steady and hard as nails
knocks at the first plum blossoms
to brush February's dull grey.
All winter I have come to this empty house
in mid-afternoon, to this quiet,
begging to be silenced by you.
I cook dinner at three,
blinding the windows with steam,
or bury myself in books
fighting the impulse to curl into a seed
dormant until your return.
Occasionally, I rouse myself to walk in the rain
past the gully, the alder's red haze
decorated by ghost globes of nests
and last year's purple clematis flowers.
Each morning it is more difficult
to face the round of emptiness and desire.
One dawn they will find us,
our legs spiralled as morning glory,
our bellies warm,
and our eyelids fluttering,
a rippling sheen of birds.

The windows bang
as wind breathes air
in and out of the room.
opened wide by large gusts
and your barely audible breath,
I remember a storm
in the California desert.

2

She and I lived in the last house
on a dirt road that ended
in the ridged desert;
creosote, cholla cactus, prickly pear
studded the burnt arroyos.

There was no relief from heat.
We slept separate,
naked on army cots
sweating as much as we drank.
On the front porch
she let desert noises
and the small night breeze
float over her.
I slept in the back room
afraid of Coyotes, snakes,
the distant glitter.
All summer I wanted her.

At first a few drops,
hazy heat flashes,

then a thousand hairline fractures
split the night sky.

She ran naked
up the sandy wash,
lay on her back,
let fierce wind and light
and rain scour her eyes,
then hooted for Coyote
to share her excruciating joy.

I huddled, a twittering sparrow
watching the storm from a hollowed
out hole in a Joshua Tree.

3

Tonight, above the pounding rain
and thunder, I hear two branches
scrape in the wind.
I lean toward you,
your skin rose colored.
You circle near me
in your sleep.
We are two clouds jostling
each other loose.
The sky opens.

For Kim Cook

People with less pleasing lovers
walk their dogs in the bitter cold.
We see the blue crystal mountains
from your window as we turn
and turn warming your unheated room
with our wandering.
It all comes back to me:
those moments I stood on the highway's edge
in Montana, Wyoming, Utah,
kicking at gravel and glass,
bewildered and happy at the turn of fate
that left me the only breathing figure
for miles of mesas, buttes, and sandstone cliffs.
Those nights I faced the land
where the highway ended as dusk began
I slept drunk   alone   cold
under scrub bushes, wrapped in a jacket,
eyes burning with stars.
I had to will my heart to beat.

My face nuzzled in pebbled dirt
and dry grass muffled the wind
carrying the small animals' losses.
No one told me I would find
the same comfort and loss
waking, listening to your heart beat
knowing the day would break
as your finger traced my spine,
as if opening a milkweed pod, each seed

folded into itself, the wings
silken, damp, the seed tips
arranged in tiers. As we turn
and touch, your room crackles with heat.
I catch your eyes looking past me
into dark hills and I know that each hour
my heart pounded into the quiet earth
was stored in the crystal of blue mountains.

Emily Warn was born in San Francisco, spent her youth in Michigan, returned to the West Coast and now lives in Seattle. She earned a B.A. at Kalamazoo College and an M.A. at the University of Washington. She has worked as a teacher and for the National Park Service. This is her first volume of poetry.

A Note on the Type

This book is composed in 12 point Perpetua, a typeface designed by Eric Gill in 1929 for the Monotype Corporation. Gill's long experience in stonecutting is reflected in the inscriptional quality of the letterforms. Typesetting by Irish Setter.